FEARLESS

Standing firm when the going gets tough

Jonty Allcock

Fearless: standing firm when the going gets tough
© Jonty Allcock/The Good Book Company 2014

Published by
The Good Book Company
Tel (UK): 0333 123 0880;
International: +44 (0) 208 942 0880
Email: info@thegoodbook.co.uk

Websites:
UK: www.thegoodbook.co.uk
North America: www.thegoodbook.com
Australia: www.thegoodbook.com.au
New Zealand: www.thegoodbook.co.nz

Unless indicated, all Scripture references are taken from the HOLY BIBLE, NEW
INTERNATIONAL VERSION. Copyright © 1973, 1978, 1984, 2011 International Bible
Society. Used by permission.

ISBN: 9781909919822

Printed in the UK

Design and illustration by André Parker

Contents

Introduction

This is the true story of one man who held his nerve and stood firm.

He faced powerful temptations, vicious enemies, formidable kings and ravenous lions. Yet for seventy years he stood his ground.

How did he do it? He wasn't a superhero. It wasn't because he had great willpower or showed extreme bravery.

It's because he knew God.

His name was Daniel—and he was totally convinced that God is the only King worth living for.

Do you know God like that?

That's what this book is all about. We're going to meet the God who makes life worth living. We're going to learn about Jesus, who came so that we can know God personally.

It's only knowing God that will make us courageous. It's only knowing God that will enable us to say "no" to temptation. It's only knowing God that will last for ever.

Are you ready to meet him?

Chapter One:
Changing sides

But Daniel resolved not to defile himself with the royal food and wine.   Daniel 1 v 8

Please read Daniel chapter 1

Sometimes I feel sorry for my phone. The truth is I'm not very loyal, so I'm constantly looking around for something better. I hate being locked into a contract for two years—I want the freedom to change team; to shop around; to upgrade. My loyalty only lasts for as long as it suits me.

So I feel sorry for my phone.

But supposing this changing-phone mentality spilled over into other areas of life. My friendships? My family? The way I treat God? Supposing I only stayed loyal for as long as it suited me; always waiting for a better offer.

Makes you wonder.

Where does the loyalty of our hearts really lie? That's the searching question that confronts us as we dig into this book of Daniel.

There are basically two options. **There are two kingdoms and we all belong to one or the other.** We're either loyal citizens of the *kingdom of God* or we're loyal subjects of the *kingdom of the world*.

The kingdom of God

If we're going to understand the book of Daniel, we have to get our heads round these two kingdoms. The story of our world is a story of these two kingdoms.

It all starts with a very powerful King. His name is God and he created all things. He spoke and it all came into being: the sun, the moon, the stars and planet earth.

And God had a great plan for the earth. It wasn't just another planet floating in space—God created earth to be his kingdom. It was a beautiful place, where people lived and God ruled as King. With God as King, it was safe; with God as King, there were good things to enjoy.

Security. Satisfaction. Sorted. That's the *kingdom of God*.

This is crucial. Do you see where the *kingdom of God* is located? Not in some heavenly place far, far away—it's on earth. That was always the plan for the *kingdom of God*.

The kingdom of the world

But then another kingdom appeared. Human beings rejected God as King and established a new kingdom on earth—a rival kingdom—the *kingdom of the world*. God's good word is ignored and human beings rule. (Read all about it in Genesis 3.) People always think that getting rid of God will bring freedom but instead it has brought death and disaster.

Fighting. Frustration. Fear. That's the *kingdom of the world*.

Two kingdoms. And they are at war.

Throughout history God has been at work to establish his great kingdom on earth. He has a very great plan. That's the great story of the Bible—from Abraham to Israel to David to Jesus—it's the story of the *kingdom of God*.

But at exactly the same time, people have been scrabbling around trying to establish the rival *kingdom of the world*. The war rages.

And so this book of Daniel challenges us. Where does our loyalty lie? What about when things get tough? Will we change sides? How do we even decide?

We live in the middle of this great battle. **Will we invest our lives in the *kingdom of God* or the *kingdom of the world*?** What are we living for?

We're going to see some pretty stunning truths about the *kingdom of God*—and expose some harsh realities about the *kingdom of the world*.

Let's get into the story.

Time to change sides?

Daniel was a man who got caught up in the crossfire of this war of kingdoms. He grew up in a place called Jerusalem. It was the capital city of God's kingdom on earth. God's temple was there—it was the place where God lived with his people. Daniel was well and truly on the side of God's kingdom.

"Great," you might think.

But then something happened that changed every-thing. It shook the very foundations of Daniel's world. Here's how the Bible describes it:

> *In the third year of the reign of Jehoiakim king of Judah, Nebuchadnezzar king of Babylon came to Jerusalem and besieged it.*   *Daniel 1 v 1*

Jerusalem is surrounded; the *kingdom of the world* is attacking. Surely God will step in and rescue. You know how it works: just when all seems lost, the great superhero swoops in and saves the day.

Except God doesn't.

The enemy comes crashing in. They smash stuff up, carry off prisoners and destroy the temple. The *kingdom of the world* seems to defeat the *kingdom of God*.

So young Daniel finds himself living in Babylon—a strange place with other gods, a new language and culture, and far from home. It would be tempting at that point for Daniel to change sides. God has let him down—he needs an upgrade.

Can you imagine the pressure? Here's the first big challenge to Daniel's loyalty.

God looks weak

God seems to have been spectacularly defeated. **Has God fallen asleep? Has God gone on vacation?** Where has he gone?

Don't you sometimes feel like that? There are times when we look around us and think that God seems weak. It looks as if God is losing. It seems that the *kingdom of God* is a foolish place in which to invest our lives; the *kingdom of the world* looks a much better place to be.

Perhaps things seem to be going wrong and we ask: "Where have you gone, God?"

We can find our loyalty wavering. But Daniel stands firm. He could see that things were not quite the way they appeared.

When Jerusalem was attacked, something bigger was going on. Something that's going to shock you. Here's what the Bible says.

> And the Lord delivered Jehoiakim king of Judah into his [Nebuchadnezzar's] hand, along with some of the articles from the temple of God. These he carried off to the temple of his god in Babylonia and put in the treasure-house of his god.
>
> Daniel 1 v 2

Why did Babylon defeat Jerusalem? Because God did it. God was not being weak; God was absolutely in control. That's a surprise. Why would God do that?

The people living in Jerusalem were supposed to be the *kingdom of God* on earth. God had rescued them and taken care of them and provided for them. And in return they had run off to find other gods. They were disloyal. **They didn't want God—they wanted an upgrade.**

So God was rightly punishing them. He wasn't weak—he was carrying out his plan. He was establishing the *kingdom of God* on earth, and was punishing those who would be disloyal.

Daniel can see that. And so he doesn't abandon God as a weakling. He remains loyal to God even when things are tough.

So here's the challenge for us. Don't give up on the *kingdom of God* just because it looks weak. God is totally in control and is working out his plan.

Strong weakness

Let me take you to another time when it looked as if the *kingdom of the world* had defeated the *kingdom of God*.

A man is dying on a wooden cross. He's covered in blood; he's crying out. His name is Jesus, and he was supposed to be the Son of God. But just look at him now—he looks so weak. God looks weak. It's the *kingdom of the world* that looks strong.

But look harder; look beyond the surface. Actually, what God is doing through the death of Jesus on the cross is his amazing plan. It's through the death of Jesus that the *kingdom of God* is established on earth. Through the blood and the pain, God will rescue millions of people and bring them into his kingdom.

Can you see it? Daniel could see what God was doing and so he stayed loyal. We have to see beyond the mess of this world to the God who is working out his plans. He will establish his kingdom.

But then comes the second massive challenge to Daniel's loyalty.

Babylon looks good

Daniel has got a lot going for him. Don't believe me? Check this out (although I warn you—it's the kind of description that might make you sick).

> Then the king ordered Ashpenaz, chief of his court officials, to bring into the king's service some of the Israelites from the royal family and the nobility—young men without any physical defect, handsome, showing aptitude for every kind of learning, well informed, quick to understand, and qualified to serve in the king's palace. He was to teach them the language and literature of the Babylonians.
>
> *Daniel 1 v 3-4*

Daniel has to be happy with that as a summary: "no physical defect". I mean, come on, that's just not fair! But anyway, back to the story.

12

Daniel gets on with life in Babylon. He begins to learn the language and the culture. His name is changed to be more Babylonian. He doesn't kick up a fuss; he gets on with it. But then we're told this:

> *The king assigned them a daily amount of food and wine from the king's table.*   Daniel 1 v 5

Hey, hey, things are looking up. Maybe Babylon is not going to be so bad after all. This is going to be fun. Let's dig in.

But Daniel makes an extraordinary decision.

> **But Daniel resolved not to defile himself with the royal food and wine, and he asked the chief official for permission not to defile himself in this way.**   Daniel 1 v 8

He'll learn the language; he'll take a new name; but he'll not eat the food. Instead he chooses to have just vegetables and water. What's that about?

Surely Daniel should be able to enjoy some of the perks of life in Babylon? But Daniel draws the line. He can see that eating this food would defile him—it would be wrong in God's eyes.

Maybe the food has been offered to other gods. We don't know. Or maybe Daniel can feel a more subtle danger. A little voice that perhaps goes something like this…

"Here is a king who can provide me with great food and wine. God has let me down. He didn't rescue me and provide for me. Why shouldn't I enjoy this stuff? At least in the kingdom of the world I can have some fun."

Do you see the danger? Maybe Daniel can feel Babylon pulling on his heart and he's fighting to stay loyal to God. He doesn't want to be defiled.

He takes a stand and refuses the king's food. That was a risky move—it's pretty offensive to refuse to eat someone's food—but Daniel knows where his loyalty lies. **Not with the King of Babylon, however tasty the meatballs.**

Wise choice

Daniel's loyalty is proved right. God takes care of Daniel and, after ten days of vegetables, he's stronger than any of the others. God gives Daniel wisdom, too.

Loyalty to God was tough, but it was proved right. When Daniel felt his heart being tugged away from God, he immediately slammed the door. He said "no". He knew where to draw the line.

I wonder if *we* know where to draw the line?

Being a Christian doesn't mean having nothing to do with the world. **We're not supposed to live in a wardrobe and ignore everyone else.** There's a lot that's good; things we can enjoy. We can learn and join in the culture around us: music, poetry, science and so on.

But some of us are very bad at drawing the line. We never really learn to say "no" to anything. We're drawn away from God by all the exciting sparkly things around us. We end up defiled. We change kingdoms.

That was my experience when I left home for the first time. I didn't know where the line was. I said "yes" to things that should have been a "no". My heart was drawn away. I wanted to upgrade my life. I wanted things to be a bit more exciting. I ended up distant from God. Then I realised what Daniel knew all along.

DO NOT DISTURB

WELCOME

Loyalty to God is key. He's the King who made us. He's the King who is in control. He's the King who is building his kingdom. To turn our back on that is madness.

So which kingdom will you invest your life in? Are there lines that you need to draw? Are there things you need to say "no" to? You won't regret it. Daniel certainly didn't.

Chapter Two:
After you

> *In the time of those kings, the God of heaven will set up a kingdom that will never be destroyed, nor will it be left to another people. It will crush all those kingdoms and bring them to an end, but it will itself endure for ever.*
>
> *Daniel 2 v 44*

Please read Daniel chapters 2 to 4

I've always had a bit of a problem with peacocks. It may be a bit harsh but they just seem so full of themselves. They know they have beautiful feathers and take any opportunity to strut their stuff. They walk around as if to say: "Look at me. I am beautiful. Be amazed, all you ugly things. It is I, the peacock."

King Nebuchadnezzar is a peacock. He's the king of Babylon and is very proud of his power and wealth. He loves to strut his stuff. **But he's about to have his tail feathers plucked.** We can read all about it in Daniel chapters 2 to 4.

Sweet dreams

It all starts with Nebuchadnezzar going to bed. He lies his head on the pillow as the most powerful man in the world. During the night he has a dream that rocks his world. Or at least it should have done—if he could understand it.

Imagine that: the most powerful man in the world and he doesn't know what his dream means.

So Nebuchadnezzar calls for *the wise guys*: the top brains of Babylon. They all come trundling in.

He wants to know what the dream means, but he's a bit paranoid. **Imagine that: the most powerful man in the world and he doesn't know who he can trust.** These wise guys can make up whatever they want about his dream. How does he know if they're just conning him?

So he set up a test. They would first have to **tell** Neb the dream; and **then explain** what it means.

Clever, huh?

Well no. Not so much clever as utterly, ridiculously impossible. No one can do that. It didn't take a wise man to see they were in

trouble. They tried to reason with the king, but he was having none of it. He ordered that they should all be killed. Just like that.

After all, what's the point of a wise man if, at the very point you need him, he can't help you?

The revealer of mysteries

Daniel belongs to *the wise guys* and so he's in the firing line and heading for the chop. But he doesn't run for cover. Instead, he asks for time so that he can interpret the dream. Is this a case of Daniel being self-confident? Not at all. **Daniel has no chance of working out the dream**, but his confidence is in God. He knows that God is able to reveal mysteries. So he prays, and God delivers.

Then Daniel goes to the king and tells him that God has revealed the dream.

This really cuts our world down to size. People often say that human beings can work everything out. We can sort the problems; we're so brilliant. But that's all peacock talk.

There is some stuff we can't work out. Nebuchadnezzar couldn't; the wise guys of Babylon couldn't; and neither can we.

But God knows all mysteries. He reveals what we could never know on our own. **We just have to be willing to listen.** Daniel was ready to admit he didn't know the answers to life. He was ready to listen. What about us?

God has given us his word, the Bible. It contains amazing truths that we could never work out for ourselves. Are we willing to listen to him? Or are we too wrapped up in our own little plans and ideas about what matters?

So Daniel goes to the king ready to reveal the dream.

Neb's dream was all about a statue. It had a head of gold, chest and arms of silver, belly and thighs of bronze, legs of iron, and feet of iron and clay. Then, in the dream, a little rock shows up. It smashes the statue to bits and grows to become a great mountain.

So far so good. Then Daniel begins to explain what the dream is all about.

It starts off well for Nebuchadnezzar. "Your Majesty ... you are that head of gold."

You can feel the peacock starting to strut. The tail feathers are coming out. Yes, Daniel, you're quite right. My kingdom is outstanding and glorious.

But wait for it. Here comes the painful bit. Two words that burst the bubble completely.

After you, another kingdom will arise…

After you.

Do you feel it? Nebuchadnezzar's kingdom of gold will be followed by another kingdom, then another, and another.

The wise men say in Daniel 2 v 4: "May the king live for ever!" But Daniel says: "After you…"

This isn't part of Nebuchadnezzar's game plan. Especially when Daniel gets to the part about the little rock. That's a kingdom that will last for ever—not like the temporary kingdom of Babylon. God has a plan to establish a kingdom that will never end.

Nebuchadnezzar is cut down to size.

Snip, snip, snip.

When you think about this, it's all so human. Let's be honest, we often act as if we'll live for ever. We like to ignore the reality of death. We either strut around thinking we're important, or **we wish we were, and try to find a way to improve our tail.**

We need to hear those two little words. "After you…"

Everything we own; everything we do; everything we achieve. There'll be an "after you".

After you, someone else will live in your house. After you, someone else will take your place. After you, someone else will be the football captain. After you, someone else will be the top of the class. After you, life will move on. And you'll be forgotten.

Do you know the names of your great, great grandparents? Didn't think so. **Only a hundred years or so and we'll be completely forgotten.**

I know it's hard to hear but we're not as important as we like to pretend we are. In the *kingdom of the world*, we're the centre of everything. In the *kingdom of God*, he's the centre of everything. That's why his kingdom lasts for ever and the *kingdom of the world* comes crashing down.

Another part of the Bible puts it like this.

> *No one remembers the former generations, and even those yet to come will not be remembered by those who follow them.*
> *Ecclesiastes 1 v 11*

Snip, snip, snip.

Can you hear the tail feathers being trimmed?

This isn't supposed to make us feel rubbish about ourselves. We're supposed to see that being part of the *kingdom of God* is what really matters.

The Rock

Daniel describes it like this:

> *In the time of those kings, the God of heaven will set up a*
> *kingdom that will never be destroyed, nor will it be left to*
> *another people. It will crush all those kingdoms and bring them to*
> *an end, but it will itself endure for ever.*
>
> *Daniel 2 v 44*

We have to get this clear. We have to learn the difference between what is temporary and what lasts for ever. Only then will we stop behaving like peacocks and start to live for what really matters.

So much of what we live for will be gone in just a few years. This is what makes the *kingdom of God* so extraordinary. And the kingdom has begun...

God's kingdom

When Jesus first began to preach, his message was:

> *The kingdom of God has come near. Repent and believe the good*
> *news!* *Mark 1 v 15*

What a claim! Jesus brings *God's kingdom*. And **this kingdom lasts for ever because its King lives for ever**. Death was not the end for King Jesus.

He died once on the cross to pay the price for sin. Then he rose to life never to die again. Here is the King who's really worth living for.

To be part of *God's kingdom* today means coming to Jesus. It means recognising that he is King. It means admitting we've lived our lives against God in the *kingdom of the world*. It means asking for forgiveness and turning to follow him.

How will Nebuchadnezzar respond to his tail clipping?

He fights back and becomes even more peacock-like. In Daniel chapter 3, Neb builds a statue. And he makes it with a head of gold. And a body of gold. And legs of gold. And feet of gold.

The message is pretty clear. There'll be no "after me". It's *my* kingdom that will outlast all others. It's *my* kingdom that will stand for ever.

In order to make the point, he orders everyone to join in worshipping this "everlasting kingdom". He gives them an anthem that will stir the soul. He gives them a bright and shiny statue that will captivate their eyes. The crowds are carried along on a patriotic wave of emotion.

And just to make sure everyone played the game, **refusal to worship was punishable by death**.

So the music sounds, and the crowds bow down.

Just three men

Daniel doesn't appear in this chapter—perhaps he was out of town. The focus shifts to three of his mates. We need to see that Daniel isn't the only one standing firm in Babylon. There are others too.

They're not fooled by the statue; they're not impressed by the music. As the anthem begins to sound, the three men stay on their feet. They're ready to stand out from the crowd. Their response is clear for everyone to see.

This is how it was reported to King Nebuchadnezzar:

There are some Jews whom you have set over the affairs of the province of Babylon—Shadrach, Meshach and Abednego—who pay no attention to you, Your Majesty. They neither serve your gods nor worship the image of gold you have set up.

Daniel 3 v 12

So what is it with these three, then? Why don't they join in with the crowds? They risk being fried for their stand. Surely they're making a huge mistake. By refusing to obey Nebuchadnezzar, they've **picked a fight with the wrong peacock**.

Or so you might think.

But they see things completely differently. They're looking to another King. A greater King. A King who makes the ninety-foot gold statue look like a shabby little *Lego* toy. They belong to the *kingdom of God*.

This is what Shadrach, Meshach and Abednego say to Nebuchadnezzar in verse 16:

King Nebuchadnezzar, we do not need to defend ourselves before you in this matter. If we are thrown into the blazing furnace, the

God we serve is able to deliver us from it, and he will deliver us from Your Majesty's hand. But even if he does not, we want you to know, Your Majesty, that we will not serve your gods or worship the image of gold you have set up.

Under the most intense pressure, these three men hold firm. They stand loyal to God. They're unshaken and unmoved. They're choosing the *kingdom of God* rather than the *kingdom of the world*.

They were not being heroic—we're not supposed to copy their bravery—they were just ordinary people like us. **But they could see the difference between the temporary and the everlasting.** They knew their God was the One true King. And that's what we must learn. If we have a flimsy view of God, then we'll cave in as soon as things hot up. But if we could see God as he really is, we would stand firm.

Take a stand

You'll face all sorts of pressure to join in with the crowd. Our world has its shiny statues that captivate our eyes, and its anthems that stir our souls. It's easy to be swept along with the crowd.

You'll stick out like a sore thumb if you don't go along with the crowd. The latest sexually-charged TV series that everyone is watching. The gossiping about the new girl at school. The short skirts and low tops that all the girls are wearing. It's tough to be different. Isn't it?

The solution isn't to try harder and be brave. Instead we need to get a fresh view of God and his kingdom. **Insults hurt, but only for a while. God's kingdom lasts for ever.** Don't miss this and get swept along with the crowd.

We really need a shift of perspective.

The three friends do get chucked into the fire. The fire is hot. It looks bad. But then, in the middle of the fire, a man turns up. He's walking around, clear as day. He keeps them safe; he brings them through. The men come out unharmed.

Who is the mystery man? It's the true King of course. The true King, who saves his people. The true King, who would one day come, not just to a fiery furnace, but to die on a cross. **It's Jesus, the King who is worth living for.**

When the pressure is on, which way will you go? Joining in with the peacocks and proudly living for a temporary kingdom? Or taking a stand because you know the King of the everlasting kingdom?

For Shad, Mesh and Abed it was a no-brainer. What about you? Where do you feel the pressure to go with the crowd? Jesus is the King who will never be replaced. God's kingdom is the only one that will never be destroyed. You know it makes sense.

Back to the peacock

So what became of Nebuchadnezzar? I haven't got time to tell you what happened in Daniel chapter 4. Let's just say his tail was completely plucked out and he finally admitted the truth. You can read it for yourselves. It's quite a story.

But now we turn to the kings that came next in Babylon. It doesn't get better. We move from peacocks to lions...

Chapter Three:
Sharp teeth

Daniel, servant of the living God, has your God, whom you serve continually, been able to rescue you from the lions?

Daniel 6 v 20

Please read Daniel chapters 5 and 6

It was a moment of extreme bravery. I was face to face with an angry leopard. It had razor sharp teeth and claws; it was crouching down and was ready to pounce; I had no doubt it wanted to kill me. I stared straight into its eyes and was determined not to run away. It snarled—I snarled back—I would not be intimidated. In a lightning fast move it leapt at me. It was coming straight for my face. And then it hit the glass. I smiled smugly.

I was safe standing outside the enclosure, but if I'd been on the other side of the glass, it would have been a very different story. It clearly wanted to kill me. One night in with that leopard would have been a terrifying experience.

In this chapter, Daniel finds himself on the wrong side of the fence, spending a night in a den of vicious lions. It's a hostile, dangerous place to be. **Forget cute and cuddly—more violent and hungry.**

But that one night with the lions is like the whole of Daniel's experience in Babylon. It was a hostile and dangerous place to be. He lived in enemy territory. It wasn't just one night—**Daniel spent seventy years living in a lion's den.**

As a teenager, Daniel had been snatched out of Jerusalem. That was *God's kingdom*, the place of security and safety. He was transported to Babylon: a *hostile kingdom*. It was a tough and stressful place to live. Danger and enemies were all around; prowling lions wanting to take him down.

Not just Daniel

The Bible says our world is like a lion's den. The *kingdom of this world* is a hostile and dangerous place. There's an enemy who wants to destroy us. His name is the devil and this is how he's described:

> *Your enemy the devil prowls around like a roaring lion looking for someone to devour.*   *1 Peter 5 v 8*

Just as children's books like to reduce lions to cute and fluffy, our world has reduced the devil to a comic-book character who is fun-loving and a bit naughty.

People dismiss the idea of a devil as old-fashioned and ridiculous. But the Bible shows it differently. **There's a dangerous enemy and he has sharp teeth.**

We're going to look closely at Daniel's experience in the "lion's den" of Babylon. And then we'll see how Jesus experienced the same thing when he came and lived in the "lion's den" of this world. That will help us to understand what life will be like for those who choose to stand firm and live for *God's kingdom* today.

Got it? **Daniel**… then **Jesus**… then **us**.

So what was life like for Daniel? We're going to think of two types of enemy that Daniel faced.

As we get to Daniel chapter 5, we discover that time has raced on. Nebuchadnezzar is dead. There'll be no more strutting for him. His son, Belshazzar, is the new kid on the throne.

And he's wasting no time in making a splash. He wants to show off to the world his extravagant lifestyle. One thousand A-list celebrities are invited; the wine is flowing; this is a party that pushed the limits. You get the feeling he wants to be extreme and shock his guests.

Gold cups from God's temple in Jerusalem are now used to fuel the drunkenness. Belshazzar's wickedness goes beyond that of his father.

By the way, **human sin is always like this. It's never satisfied.** There's always a need to push a little bit further. It's a dangerous and slippery road.

Whether it's partying or drugs or alcohol or pornography or money, you'll always find that as time goes by you need to do more and go further to get the same effect. Can you see that in your life? Are there boundaries that you're pushing in order to impress your friends or find satisfaction? Beware, it's a dangerous road you're travelling.

Anyway, Belshazzar is about to get the shock of his life. Check out what happened:

> Suddenly the fingers of a human hand appeared and wrote on the plaster of the wall, near the lampstand in the royal palace. The king watched the hand as it wrote. His face turned pale and he was so frightened that his legs became weak and his knees were knocking.   Daniel 5 v 5-6

A message on a wall—secret writing that no one could understand. It made no sense. So Belshazzar called for *the wise guys* to read it for him. Guess what? They couldn't understand it. **The standard of**

"wise guy" in Babylon had not improved since his dad's day. Belshazzar was in trouble.

On the shelf

Don't panic—the queen has a plan. She suggests they ask Daniel.

But here comes the shocker. Belshazzar's response is basically: "Who is Daniel?"

Daniel has been completely ignored. He's been put on a shelf. He's a forgotten nobody in Babylon. Despite all he did in the days of Nebu-chadnezzar, this king doesn't even know his name.

That must have been tough, don't you think? This is the reality of life in the lion's den. That's life in the *kingdom of the world*. Here's the enemy who just ignores Daniel. He gets on with his partying and Daniel gets forgotten.

Daniel isn't hated, or beaten up, or abused. He's just ignored.

It's tragic. **Belshazzar has access to the wisest man in the whole world, and he doesn't even know his name.** Wow. Sin increases while wisdom is forgotten.

Eventually, Daniel is found and comes into the middle of the party. He reads the mystery writing and the message isn't good. Belshazzar knew all about how his dad was humbled by God. He knew all about Daniel's wisdom. But he had proudly ignored it and got on with his own little party. God is rightly angry at the arrogance.

Belshazzar is going to die. His kingdom is going to be divided up and given to others. His time is up.

Daniel is God's messenger to Belshazzar. God is giving him a chance to change.

How will Belshazzar react? It's unbelievable, but he completely ignores what God has said. He lavishes gifts on Daniel, but he changes nothing. He does nothing. He does not listen.

So the Bible tells us:

> *That very night Belshazzar, king of the Babylonians, was slain, and Darius the Mede took over the kingdom, at the age of sixty-two.*
> *Daniel 5 v 30*

Game over.

Belshazzar made a disastrous mistake. **He ignored the message of God and chose to live for ever-increasing sin.**

He didn't hate Daniel; he just ignored him. That's the first type of enemy.

And Jesus faced this enemy too.

Jesus who?

When Jesus walked the earth, there were many who simply ignored him. They dismissed him as irrelevant and unimportant. On one oc-

31

casion (in Mark 5 v 14-17) Jesus healed a man, and then the whole town asked him to go away. They preferred to carry on life without Jesus.

And people still treat Jesus that way today.

Many in our world would say they don't hate Jesus. They just ignore him.

It's a tragedy. **He's the wisest man who has ever lived, and people don't even know his name.** Daniel chapter 5 shows us that to ignore Jesus is to be his enemy.

We're surrounded by those who ignore Jesus. Partying hard. It's far easier just to go with the flow. Jesus can wait for another time. There's wine to be drunk and fun to be had. The devil loves to convince us that Jesus is irrelevant. We don't have to hate him; we can just sideline him—put him to one side and carry on.

Hear the warning. Jesus came so that you can know God. We've all made mistakes. But Jesus came so we can be forgiven for the wrong we've done. Jesus came so we can be part of *God's everlasting kingdom*.

By ignoring Jesus, we make ourselves God's enemies. We don't have to hate him; we just have to ignore him. It's that serious.

And us...?

People treated Daniel that way. They treated Jesus that way. And if we belong to Jesus, they may well treat *us* that way too.

If we belong to *God's kingdom*, there'll be times when we're ignored. The party goes on and we're left on the shelf. It feels rubbish, doesn't it? It's how the enemy works. But the party of the world will be cut short. The real power lies with *God's kingdom*.

So, Daniel stood firm. And Jesus stood firm. **Are we ready to stand firm in the face of the enemy?**

With the death of Belshazzar the enemy changes. Here comes the second type of enemy.

The enemies that roar

If Daniel is pretty much ignored in chapter 5, then he takes centre stage in chapter 6. The new king (called Darius) is impressed by Daniel.

> *Now Daniel so distinguished himself among the chief ministers and the satraps (local rulers) by his exceptional qualities that the king planned to set him over the whole kingdom.*
>
> *Daniel 6 v 3*

Daniel must be getting pretty old by now. He's been in enemy territory for somewhere near seventy years. But he isn't ready to sit down and give up. He's still doing the best he can—working hard, doing the right thing. Things are looking good; but don't be fooled—the lions are circling.

> *At this, the chief ministers and the satraps tried to find grounds for charges against Daniel in his conduct of government affairs, but they were unable to do so.* *Daniel 6 v 4*

The claws are out. They're jealous and want to take Daniel down. So they come up with a plan. They tell the king to make a law that for thirty days people can only pray to him and no one else. King Darius likes the sound of that. He can't see what they're doing and so he passes the law. If anyone breaks this law, **they will become lion food**.

Daniel once again faces a choice. He could just keep his praying secret and try to stay out of trouble. Or he could obey the law and save his life. But instead he does this:

> *Now when Daniel learned that the decree had been published, he went home to his upstairs room where the windows opened towards Jerusalem. Three times a day he got down on his knees and prayed, giving thanks to his God, just as he had done before.*

Daniel 6 v 10

Daniel isn't going to hide away. He knows where his confidence lies. Not in the *kingdom of this world*, but in the *kingdom of God*.

He would rather be fed to lions than disobey God.

The enemies are watching and, as soon as Daniel prays, they run off to the king. They're like little school-children telling tales. *Daniel is praying! Daniel is praying!*

King Darius is devastated—he has been conned. He tries to save Daniel, but he can't break his word. What a pointless king. He's not able to save Daniel.

Just as well Daniel has got his trust in another King.

When the enemies are accusing Daniel and lying about him, Daniel says… nothing. He's silent. He's not trying to save himself. Daniel has his trust in another King.

So Daniel is chucked in with the lions and the cave is sealed. The king can't sleep. Early in the morning he runs to the cave. The stone is rolled away and King Darius says:

Daniel, servant of the living God, has your God, whom you serve continually, been able to rescue you from the lions?

Oh yes! God is the King who saves. God shut the mouths of the lions. Daniel had his confidence in the right King. He's safe. Daniel is lifted out and the enemies are thrown in. Daniel made a wise choice.

The point is pretty clear. **In a dangerous world you need to find yourself a King who really has the power to save you.** And then you need to remain loyal to that King no matter what.

That King's name is Jesus. (If you're wondering how that's possible— because we've just learned from Daniel that "*God* is the King who saves"—all will be explained in the next chapter.)

Jesus and lions

Daniel experienced the lion's den. **And so did Jesus.**

Jesus left heaven, a place of security and safety. He came and lived in enemy territory. He was lied about, and yet remained silent. He was trusting his Father, the King.

At his trial, the Roman governor, Pilate, tried to set Jesus free. But couldn't. Another ruler who could not save. Jesus went to the cross. It was as if he was torn apart by lions.

His dead body was placed in a cave and a stone sealed the entrance. Then, early one Sunday morning, some women ran to the tomb and discovered the most amazing fact in all history.

God shut the mouth of death itself. Jesus was alive. Here is a King worth trusting.

So when life is tough, don't give up. When people attack you, don't lash out and retaliate. Some people will hate you if you choose to belong to *God's kingdom*. People will look for ways to take you down. People will oppose you and make life hard for you. When that happens, you need to know there's a King who can save you. Don't put your hope in human saviours (friends, boyfriends, politicians, whatever). They will turn out to be useless.

It is King Jesus alone who can save us.

Will you trust him even in the face of the lions? Will you hold your nerve and stand firm?

Chapter Four:
Look beyond

*In my vision at night I looked, and there before me was one like a
son of man, coming with the clouds of heaven.*

Daniel 7 v 13

Please read Daniel 7

I was a pretty sensitive six-year-old. I still remember an experience
that left me deeply scarred. I was with a big crowd of people watching a man driving his car. As he drove along, one of the doors just
fell off. Completely. Then the other one. People around me were
laughing. I couldn't believe it—this guy was having a nightmare.
Then the wheels came off, the engine exploded and the whole thing
fell to bits. But no one in the crowd seemed at all concerned. I was
freaking out.

Of course, what I didn't realise was that this guy was a clown and
his car was supposed to fall apart. (Looking back, the red nose and
green wig should have given me a clue.)

That was my problem. I could see what was happening—but I
couldn't really *see* what was happening. Do you get my point?

That's often our problem with life in this world. We see stuff happening all around us—hard things, sad things, confusing things. It can
stress us out and crush us.

But we need God's help to really see what is going on.

That's how Daniel managed to stand firm for those seventy years in Babylon. He could see beyond the enemies and lions and lies and fire. He could see things differently. That's what we're going to discover next in the book of Daniel.

A bit weird

In Daniel chapter 7, everything changes. It all goes a bit strange. No more stories—but lots of visions and beasts and angels and other weird-sounding things. What's going on?

This is called "apocalyptic" writing. Don't be impressed—it just means we're being shown some stuff that we could never see with our own eyes. **The curtain is pulled back and we're shown what's really going on behind the scenes in this world.**

My kids love to play "I spy with my little eye". But they seem to play an extreme version. Instead of picking something they can actually see, they just think of anything they like, whether they can see it or not. It's not quite the point but there we go.

The great thing about the Bible is that it really does reveal to us things that we cannot spy with our little eyes. It reveals what we could never discover for ourselves. That annoys some people because we like to think we can work it all out. But we can't. We need to lose the arrogance and humbly ask God to show us what we cannot see for ourselves.

Let's get into Daniel chapter 7 and you'll see what I mean.

In my vision at night I looked, and there before me were the four winds of heaven churning up the great sea. Four great beasts, each different from the others, came up out of the sea.

Daniel 7 v 2-3

Daniel sees a vision; try and picture it in your minds. It's supposed to be dramatic. Can you see the churning sea, roaring and foaming? Can you see four beasts emerging from the sea?

Each of the four beasts is like a terrifying animal. The first is like a lion with the wings of an eagle. The second is a bear with ribs in its mouth. The third is a leopard, and the fourth is unlike anything Daniel has seen before. Terrifying, frightening and very powerful.

On this fourth beast are ten horns, and then one more horn grows.
Why the obsession with horns?

Horns mean power. Imagine you're facing a rhino. When it charges straight for you, what does it use to lead the attack? Does it reverse at top speed with its backside? No, of course not. It lowers its head, points its horn and charges. All the power and strength of the rhino is focused on that one point. **The horn is the concentration of power.**

So four powerful beasts, one after another, with all the power concentrated into ten horns, and then into one.

What does all this mean?

We don't have to guess. Daniel is told what the beasts are all about, and, if you have your brain switched on, this might sound vaguely familiar.

The four great beasts are four kings that will rise from the earth.
Daniel 7 v 17

Power abused

In the Bible, "the sea" is often used as a picture of evil (for example in Psalm 124). It's a great image of the *kingdom of the world*. A scary and uncertain place. Here is what Daniel needs to know. In this churning world, there'll be kings and kingdoms that rise up and take power.

But the problem with power is that it's like a drug. Humans take power and abuse it. These kings are like beasts that crush and devour.

We've all seen examples of the powerful bullying the weak. In the playground, in the workplace, in families, or between nations on the world stage.

This world is a place where power is abused. It's like a churning and uncertain ocean. Have you ever experienced that? Have you ever known what it's like for someone to abuse their power over you? It's a terrifying thing. It would be easy to give up and lose hope.

Sometimes individuals arise through world history who become a concentration of that abusive power. Particular people who do massive harm in this world. Like the one horn in Daniel's vision. Doesn't it sometimes feel as if humans run the show and God is out of the picture?

This is where we need to look harder and ask God to help us to really *see* what is happening in this world.

Power limited

Scary as these beasts are, each of them comes to an end. There's an "After you…" They're terrifying, and then they're gone.

Did you ever play the chocolate game? You sit round and roll a dice. If you get a six, you put on a hat, scarf, and gloves and then have to eat chocolate with a knife and fork until someone else gets a six. It's seriously stressful. You just get yourself organised and someone else screams "six" and starts ripping the scarf from your neck. Your time is over. **It's a terrible way to eat chocolate.**

It feels like that for these human kingdoms. They get a little while in charge and then it's over. No kingdom on earth will last. No human can go on abusing their power for ever. They will become weak. Here is what Daniel saw about the bullies of this world. They're not quite as strong as they thought they were. Someone else rolls a six and their time is up.

Shhhhhh!

Then suddenly everything changes in the vision. Listen to this:

> As I looked, thrones were set in place, and the Ancient of Days
> took his seat.   Daniel 7 v 9

Above all the chaos and the churning... Above the boasting and the raging... Above the noise and the mayhem... Suddenly everything goes quiet. *Shhh.* Can you hear it?

There's a throne. And God himself takes his seat. He's the Ancient of Days. In our culture, to call someone ancient is a bit of an insult. It won't win you any friends.

But when you remember the kingdoms that have come and gone, when you remember the beasts that are short lived... To be ancient is a stunning thing. **Here is the One who outlives and outlasts them all.** Are you looking with Daniel at this magnificent God? Do you know him?

He is beautiful. He's seated. He's not stressed. He's pure. He's wise. He's awesome. He is in control.

But don't stop now. Keep looking. Something is happening. Someone is entering the royal court. It's someone who looks "like a son of man" (v 13). Here is a man and he's approaching the throne. Look what happens:

> He was given authority, glory and sovereign power; all nations
> and peoples of every language worshipped him. His dominion is
> an everlasting dominion that will not pass away, and his kingdom
> is one that will never be destroyed.
>   Daniel 7 v 14

So different to the beasts. This man doesn't grab power for himself—he is given it. He doesn't have a temporary kingdom—he has a kingdom that will never be destroyed.

This is what Daniel saw. But Daniel did not know who the man was. Imagine him trying to work it out. Who is this man who is given all authority? Who is this man who is worshipped like God? *Who is it?*

A few hundred years later, in Bethlehem, that man was born. Jesus often referred to himself as "the Son of Man". Now we know why. He's saying: "I am the man Daniel saw in his vision". This is so cool.

The Son of Man does not grab power for himself. In fact, look what Jesus did with all power.

> *Jesus knew that the Father had put all things under his power, and that he had come from God and was returning to God; so he got up from the meal, took off his outer clothing, and wrapped a towel round his waist. After that, he poured water into a basin and began to wash his disciples' feet, drying them with the towel that was wrapped round him.*
>
> John 13 v 3-5

Jesus has ALL POWER—and so he washed His disciples' feet. Wow! Here is what Jesus does with all power.

Jesus has ALL POWER—and so he went to a cross to die. He could have destroyed his enemies, but instead he allowed himself to suffer. He knew it was the only way we could be saved. He used his power to serve us.

To the human eye it looks as if the cross is the defeat of Jesus. But Jesus can see beyond. He can see more clearly. He can see what's really going on. He knows that his death is the only way for God's enemies to become his friends. So Jesus willingly goes to die as the all-powerful King.

And God's response was to raise Jesus from the dead and to GIVE HIM the name that's above every name. Jesus did not grab it—it was given to him.

Stop grabbing

All around us, people are desperately trying to grab power for themselves. We all do it in our own little ways. In fact, we're encouraged to do it. Go for it. Grab as much as you can. Push yourself forward. Be the best.

But here's the problem. **If we live like that, we'll be part of the churning sea.** We'll spend our lives looking over our shoulders. Always wondering when someone will scream "six" and we'll be pushed aside.

How about we look beyond the churning world? How about we look to Jesus? When we see Jesus, we're set free from the churning race to grab power. Instead, we can learn to serve others. When we realise that Jesus went to die on a cross for us, it will enable us to be willing to give ourselves for the good of others.

If you know the terrifying reality of this power-abusing world, then don't give up. Look beyond. Look to Jesus. He suffered so you can have life. He rose from death so that you can have hope. This churning sea will one day be finished. The *kingdom of Jesus* will never end.

But there's more we need to see about the world in which we live. Horns, goats, rams. It all kicks off in chapter 8. See you there in a minute…

Chapter Five:
Just one slice

I looked up, and there before me was a ram with two horns, standing beside the canal, and the horns were long. One of the horns was longer than the other but grew up later.

Daniel 8 v 3

Please read Daniel 8

I love eating apple pie. I'm not fussy; I'll eat pretty much any apple pie, but I want to share a secret with you. It's a principle I've developed over a number of years of apple-pie munching and that I share with you now. I think it's pretty profound. Here it is:

In order to discover the quality of an apple pie, you do not have to eat the whole pie.

Unbelievable, hey? It's what I call the "one-slice-whole-pie principle".

When approaching a new apple pie, I only need one slice to judge its sweetness, its soggy-ness and its texture. One slice provides all the information I need. **One slice unlocks the secrets of the whole pie.**

The great thing about this profound secret is that it can be used for more things than just apple-pie eating. In fact, I want to suggest that the one-slice-whole-pie (OSWP) principle is the key to understanding Daniel chapter 8. Let me explain…

We're going to read about one slice of human history. It's about some kings and their kingdoms from thousands of years ago. At first sight, it's going to seem irrelevant to us today.

But now the OSWP principle helps us out. As we look at this *one slice* of human history, it will help us to understand the *whole* of human history. What happens in this slice is repeated over and over again throughout all time.

In particular, **this slice of pie will help us to know how to stand firm when things go bad**.

Getting away with it

Don't you sometimes get annoyed when bad people get away with bad stuff? Perhaps you try and do the right thing, and your life goes wrong. But others do the wrong thing, and it all seems to go right for them.

Evil people getting away with evil things. It's a big problem in our world.

We've all been told that "honesty is the best policy" but sometimes it doesn't feel like it. I remember times as a child when I got away with stuff by telling a few lies. Like the time I broke a plate that my parents had been given for their wedding. I carefully put it back in the cupboard, and the next person who found it thought they had broken it.

I did something wrong and got away with it. **Haven't you?**

We see it on our news all the time: evil people doing evil things and having a great life. We can begin to lose our nerve. What's the point? Why bother? We might as well live for ourselves and grab as much as we can. What is God up to? It looks as if he's losing. He's too weak. He's being overpowered by evil.

Daniel 8 is going to help us to see things differently. It's going to give us a clear view of the reality of evil. And what we learn from this one slice of history will help us understand the slice we're living in.

What Daniel saw

Our first job is to get clear what Daniel saw. He's still in Babylon, and he is given a vision from God. He's shown what is going to happen in the next chunk of human history after him. It isn't pretty.

First up, there's a ram with two horns. It goes charging round the place smashing everyone up and becoming very powerful. It has some **serious anger issues** and destroys everything in its path.

But then comes a goat. This has one horn and it attacks the ram, knocks him to the ground and tramples him. *Bye-bye, Rambo.* So now we've got a goat, and it's just as bad as the ram. But its horn gets broken off and four horns grow up. And then, from one of the four horns, another horn grows. Got it?

So now we've got this one horn and we hit rock bottom. It attacks heaven itself, reaching up to the starry host. It stands against God. It tramples on God's temple. It doesn't get worse than this.

Got it? **Ram, goat, one horn, four horns, one horn.** Easy.

The great news is that Daniel is told what this all means. He's told it's all about some stuff that's about to happen on the world stage. Daniel didn't know all the names—but we can look back and see how it all worked out.

Hold onto your seats, we're going to do some history...

The ram with two horns is the Persian empire, which had two powerful kings. They were nasty and went around the place smashing everyone up. They thought they were invincible.

Until they got hit side on from an angry goat kingdom. That's the kingdom of Greece. (Don't be impressed with my historical knowledge—we're told that in verse 21.)

Remember the goat starts off with one horn? That was the first king of Greece, who was called Alexander the Great. He destroyed the Persian empire and became very powerful very quickly. But he was cut down at the age of 32, just as Daniel had seen. And the Greek empire was given to four kings—don't worry about their names. But then came the final horn Daniel saw—the worst one of all.

He was a bloke called Antiochus Epiphanes. **Cool name. Nasty bloke.** Became very powerful; and then was destroyed.

What Daniel saw all came true in history.

But so what? Who cares about goats and kings and all that? Remember the OSWP principle? *That* slice of pie helps us understand *our* slice of pie.

Evil increases

Through Daniel 8 we see evil intensifying. It gets worse and worse. One horn is followed by a worse horn until you get to the final horn, who tries to attack heaven itself. Truth is trampled; God's people are smashed.

You see that in every slice of human history. Humans taking their stand against God. People attacking God. Evil increasing.

There'll always be people who hate God's truth. There'll always be people who hate God's church. There'll be times when it looks as if evil is winning and God is losing. When Jesus came into the world, people hated him and killed him. You might think that God was trying to be nice, but that evil was too strong.

It would be easy to despair and think that God is a loser. Poor old God, sitting in heaven while all these nasty people say nasty things about him.

Do you feel as if God is losing? **Perhaps you look at our culture today and see that God is increasingly on the sidelines**—people ignore him, or attack him, or say he's irrelevant.

It looks as if God is fighting a losing battle. Evil is growing; churches are shrinking. You hold back from living for God because who wants to join up with a loser?

But come back to Daniel 8—I need you to see something very important about that slice of pie. Evil is increasing but...

Evil is controlled

Look carefully at what we're told about the final horn that comes along.

> *He will become very strong, but not by his own power.*

> *Daniel 8 v 24*

There's something more going on here. It might look as if these evil kings hold all the power, but actually **someone else is holding the real power**.

You find it again in verse 25. Here's how this final king meets his end:

Yet he will be destroyed, but not by human power.

However powerful people might become, they do not have ultimate power. There's a power beyond them; a power that controls them. That's God. We've already seen in Daniel 7 that he's the One sitting on the throne of heaven. Certainly not a loser.

I remember once watching a dog that was on a long lead. The lead was attached to a spike that was firmly attached to the ground. The dog could run around and bark and attack anything it liked. But only so far. **Once the lead ran out, the dog came to a sudden (and comical) stop.**

There was a bird that had got it worked out. It sat just out of the dog's reach and tweeted the bird equivalent of "ner-ner". The dog came tearing towards it to rip it apart and, just as it was about to strike, it was stopped in its tracks. It did not have ultimate control. It was on a lead.

That's what we need to understand about evil in our world. It may look like as if it's out of control, **but God has it on a lead**. When an evil person becomes strong, it's because of *God's* power, not *theirs*.

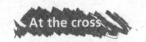
When Jesus was killed on a cross, it was not the great triumph of evil. Someone else held the real power.

When Jesus was on trial, he looked Pilate in the eye and told him:

> *You would have no power over me if it were not given to you from above.* John 19 v 11

God was not *losing* when Jesus died. God was *winning*. He was in absolute control even as evil tried its worst.

You have to understand that evil is under God's control. **He's working out his plans even through the evil that people do.** We might not understand why God would give power to evil people, but it changes everything when we know that he's still holding the lead.

God isn't pleased with evil. He's not happy about evil things that have been done to you by others. But he's in control of evil. He's the ultimate power; the only firm place to stand in a sea of evil.

God is no loser. Don't be fooled. It was true in the Daniel-8 slice of pie. It's true in our slice of pie. It's true in every slice of pie.

But Daniel needs to understand one final thing about evil…

Evil ends

Knowing the ending can really spoil a good film.

But knowing the ending of evil can really transform our lives in this world.

Daniel is told that he needs to understand that his vision "concerns the time of the end".

Evil has an end. In fact, Daniel is told the number of days until this evil ends and the evil king is brought down. 2,300 evenings and mornings. That's how much God is in control. He knows the day—it's in his calendar. There's an appointed time; and then evil ends.

God isn't waiting to see what will happen. He has already set the day. He'll bring the evil kingdom to an end and the temple will be rebuilt.

And remember the OSWP principle. In every slice of human history God brings evil to an end.

He sets the day when it will all stop. When evil people rise up against God, their end is already set. Whether it's Hitler or Bin Laden or a murderer or rapist or whoever, God knows their end. It's set by God.

The end

And God has set a final day when all evil will end.

> *For he has set a day when he will judge the world with justice by the man he has appointed. He has given proof of this to everyone by raising him from the dead.*
>
> *Acts 17 v 31*

If you know something is going to end, it helps you to persevere through the suffering.

You may be going through really rubbish stuff. You may be experiencing evil from people. You may wonder if God is bothered. You may feel that God doesn't care. Or that he's too weak to do anything.

The Daniel-8 slice of pie helps us understand our slice. Evil is controlled by God, and he has set a day when it will end.

Hold on. Stand firm. Don't despair.

Where do you feel as if God is losing right now? In the world? In your life? Where do you fee as if evil is out of control? Do you feel tempted to give up on God as a loser?

You need to learn from our Daniel-8 slice of pie. We should expect that evil will *increase*. We must know that evil is *controlled*. And we can be sure that **all evil will end**.

Why not talk to God about it now? That's what Daniel does in chapter 9…

Chapter Six:
Daniel's secret weapon

Lord, listen! Lord, forgive! Lord, hear and act! For your sake, my God, do not delay, because your city and your people bear your Name.   *Daniel 9 v 19*

Please read Daniel 9

I find praying hard. I know I'm supposed to pray. I know I need to pray. But it never seems to be very easy. Is it just me? My mind wanders off to what I was watching last night, or I suddenly need to check *Facebook*—you know how it works. Then I'm not sure what to pray about, so I just think about some people and ask God to bless them. And at the end of it all, I find it hard to know if there was really any point. Has anything actually changed?

If you know that struggle, if you've faced the same questions, then you need Daniel chapter 9. Daniel was a man who prayed. We've already seen that. **Even when he was threatened with lions... he kept on praying.**

But now we get the chance to listen in, to find out how he prayed. In this bit of Daniel we discover one of his prayers written out in full. If we listen carefully, we'll be able to hear Daniel praying. It's going to be inspiring.

There are going to be days when being part of *God's kingdom* is really tough. It might seem like a pointless waste of time.

This is why we need to learn to pray. Let me say that again as strongly as I can. We MUST learn to pray. It isn't a hobby that some people find helpful. It isn't a technique that some people master. It's the only way to get things clear and see the *kingdom of the world* for what it really is.

That's what Daniel discovered in Babylon. Don't you think there were bad days when Daniel felt like giving up? Don't you think there were times when Daniel felt afraid? Or tired? How did he stand firm?

Not because of his strength and bravery. But because he prayed. **Daniel was weak, but he knew how to pray.**

Everyone loves to be independent. We hate admitting that we need help. It's why lots of teenagers are desperate to learn to drive. I remember the day I passed my test and drove on my own for the first time. **I was free. I didn't need anyone. I was independent.** It was awesome. (Until half an hour later when I hit another car and needed Dad to help me pay for the damage…)

We want to stand on our own two feet. Destiny is

in our hands. We don't need anyone. We can do whatever we want to do. Independence.

And that's how we treat God. We assume we don't need him. But here's the thing: **we were never designed to be independent creatures**.

God is the Ruler, not us. God is the Creator and we're his creatures. We were created by God to live dependently upon him. That's why prayer is so important. It's saying to God: "Please help me. I need you."

Learning to pray is learning to understand the world properly. It's learning that God is God and we're not. It's learning that we need God, and he doesn't need us. If you've never learned to pray, don't you think it's about time?

In this prayer that Daniel prayed, there are four big things that will inspire us to pray more.

First, be inspired by…

God's great plan

Before Daniel starts to pray, he's reading the Bible. The really cool thing is that we know what he was reading. It's another part of the Bible called Jeremiah. It was written by a man called Jeremiah about seventy years earlier—just before Daniel and his mates were carried off into Babylon.

This is what the LORD says: "When seventy years are completed for Babylon, I will come to you and fulfil my good promise to bring you back to this place. For I know the plans I have for you," declares the LORD, "plans to prosper you and not to harm you, plans to give you hope and a future. Then you will call on me and come and pray to me, and I will listen to you.
Jeremiah 29 v 10-12

God promised that there would be seventy years in Babylon; and then he would bring his people back to Jerusalem. What a day that would be! The pain and suffering of Babylon would be over. Daniel reads the words, and looks at his wall chart. He counts up the years, and he sees it has been seventy years.

But he doesn't just sit back and wait for God to do what he promised. Daniel starts to pray. **He gets involved with God's great plan.** He begins to pray that God will do what he said.

Daniel isn't just praying about the things in his life that he wants God to fix. He isn't telling God his brilliant ideas about what God should do next. Instead, he prays in the light of God's great plan.

Daniel knows that he needs God to act. It's God's plan, and only God can fulfil it. So Daniel prays.

We've got prayer so messed up in our thinking. We come up with an idea that we would like—and then we ask God to do it for us. That's all wrong.

Prayer isn't about me trying to get God involved in my little plans. It's about God allowing me to be involved in his cosmic plan.

It isn't me telling God my bright ideas. It's me responding to his great idea.

One of the reasons we find it so hard to pray is that we have far too small a view of God's plan for this world. We need to do what Daniel did and read the Bible. God has an awesome plan for this world. Do you know what it is?

Through Jesus, God is gathering people together from all over the world. He's forgiving their sin; he's giving them new life; he's transforming them. It's happening today, right now, all over the world.

Near the end of the Bible, in Revelation 7, we get a glimpse of where this plan is heading.

One day there'll be people gathered up from every tribe and nation and language, and they will all be gathered together. They will stand before the great throne of God and see Jesus face to face. **All the pain and suffering of this tough and evil world will be finished.**

Are you part of the plan? Are you part of the people that God is gathering? If you are, then here's something worth praying about. Read more about the plan. Get along to church and listen to what is being preached. And as you hear more, then pray more.

Find out what's happening in God's church around the world today. Could you go and visit someone from your church who has gone overseas? Be inspired to pray by the greatness of God's plan. The more we know the plan, the more we'll pray.

But the second lesson for us to learn from Daniel's prayer is the need for…

Ruthless honesty

Daniel doesn't come to God with a list of excuses. He just admits the truth.

> *Lord, the great and awesome God, who keeps his covenant of love with those who love him and keep his commandments, we have sinned and done wrong. We have been wicked and have rebelled; we have turned away from your commands and laws.*
> *Daniel 9 v 4-5*

And that isn't the end of it. Daniel goes on in great detail about the sin of God's people, which meant they ended up in Babylon.

Daniel faces up to the truth. God gave them his law—they ignored it. God sent them prophets—they did not listen. God showed them mercy—they kicked it back in his face. **No excuses. Just the plain truth.**

We've done wrong.

Then he goes one step further. He says that God was right to punish them. That's a big thing to say.

We find it so hard to admit we're wrong. It's never our fault. We make excuses. We blame other people. And we hate to admit that we might deserve punishment.

But **if we're going to learn to pray, we need to get honest with God**. Have you ever taken time to think through the way you've treated the God who made you? Have you ever admitted it to him?

I am not talking about generally saying I'm naughty. But what about carefully and specifically thinking about the ways you haven't listened.

Will you admit that you deserve God's punishment? It's tough, isn't it? But God is right to punish sin. We deserve to be sent away from him.

We often assume we're entitled to a happy life, that it's our right to have things easy. That's nonsense. We deserve nothing from God—only punishment. Are we willing to be honest and admit it?

But Daniel doesn't end there. He prays because of his confidence in God's…

Beautiful mercy

Despite all the people have done, Daniel still comes to God and says:

> Lord, in keeping with all your righteous acts, turn away your anger and your wrath from Jerusalem, your city, your holy hill.
>
> Daniel 9 v 16

After all the wrong they have done, Daniel dares to pray: "Turn your anger away". That's an outrageous thing to pray. Except that Daniel knows what God is like. **He knows that God is full of mercy towards people who have done wrong.** That's why Daniel prays—because God is willing to turn his anger away.

Let that sink in. We deserve God's anger and his punishment. We really do. Yet, as we come to him admitting our need, his anger is turned away from us.

We've seen more of God's mercy than Daniel ever saw. We've seen how it's possible for God's anger to be turned away from us.

It's the very heart of the reason why Jesus came. The anger that I rightly deserve is turned from me and instead falls on Jesus. That's what was happening on the cross. He faced God's anger so that I might experience God's mercy.

That's how much God's mercy cost.

This is the beauty of *God's kingdom*. It's the place we find mercy.

We have to stop pretending that we don't need anyone. We have to stop pretending we don't need God. **We desperately need him.** Without his mercy we'll be sent away from his presence for ever. We'll be in the place of punishment for ever. God is absolutely right to punish sin.

But we do not have to be punished. If we admit our sin and ask for mercy, then God will be delighted to turn his anger away.

Do you see now why we MUST learn to pray?

One final thing about prayer before we move on. We need to see *why* Daniel prayed. What was really motivating him?

God's glory

Daniel doesn't ask God to act because it will make life easier. Daniel asks God to act because otherwise God will be dishonoured.

Lord, listen! Lord, forgive! Lord, hear and act! For your sake, my God, do not delay, because your city and your people bear your Name.   *Daniel 9 v 19*

Daniel hates the fact that people dishonour God. Daniel hates the fact that God's name has been trashed. That's why he prays.

Daniel prays because God is great. God is awesome—and Daniel wants the world to see.

We're mostly bothered about our glory and what people think about us. We try to build our little lives and think we don't need anyone. When we do pray, it's normally about getting God to do something nice for us. We're motivated by our own desires and ambitions. **No wonder prayer gets boring.** God doesn't play our game. So we assume prayer doesn't work, give up and just do it on our own.

I ask God to help me pass my exams so I can get a great job and make loads of money. I fail my exams. So I assume prayer doesn't work.

My praying is so often all about ME.

But that isn't the heart of praying. God isn't a fairy godmother waiting to grant our requests. He's the great and awesome God, who is worthy of our worship.

When we truly pray, we begin to see what really matters in this world. Not the shiny rubbish of the *kingdom of the world*—but the **magnificent treasure of God himself**. Why not ask God to shift your priorities? Seek his glory, not your own. Go for *his kingdom* and not the *kingdom of the world*.

That's what Daniel teaches us about how to pray. And when we learn to pray like that, we discover the secret to standing firm in a tough world.

More on the battle in the next chapter... but for now, why not pray?

Chapter Seven:
The Linen-Man

At that time I, Daniel, mourned for three weeks.

Daniel 10 v 2

Please read Daniel 10

How do you cope with bad news?

One way is to ignore it and pretend it isn't happening. You get on with shopping or drinking or partying or working. You bury the bad news and carry on.

Or there's the moping method. You push everyone else away, and find a quiet spot where you can sit on your own and feel sorry for yourself.

I was pretty good at that when I was a kid. If things were going wrong for me, I would escape down the garden and listen to sad music.

Nobody loves me,
Everybody hates me,
I'm going down the garden to eat worms.

How do *you* cope with bad news? Do you bury it or do you wallow in it? Daniel does neither. He gets some very bad news, and his response is amazing…

Daniel chapter 10 starts:

In the third year of Cyrus king of Persia...

I realise that doesn't sound very important, but it really matters. Allow me to fill in some history. (Don't switch off. Come on. It will be fun.)

Remember back in Daniel 9 it was all very exciting. The seventy years of exile in Babylon were finished. It was time for Jerusalem to be rebuilt. **Happy days.**

In the first year of King Cyrus' reign, some of God's people had left Babylon and headed back to Jerusalem. They were going to rebuild the temple. They were so full of hope; so full of excitement.

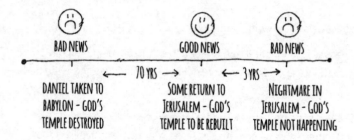

But the reality was very different. When they got back to Jerusalem, the people had a nightmare. Enemies opposed them; the new temple looked a bit small; it was all so disappointing. The people gave up. (You can read about it in Ezra chapter 4.) **Sad times.**

Meanwhile, Daniel is back in Babylon. He sees visions that tell him there's still a great struggle ahead for Jerusalem. In Daniel 10 v 1, it's described as "a great war". Things are not ok in Jerusalem. There are hard and painful days that lie ahead. How does Daniel respond to this very bad news?

At that time I, Daniel, mourned for three weeks. I ate no choice
food; no meat or wine touched my lips; and I used no lotions at all
until the three weeks were over.

Daniel 10 v 2-3

Mourning, not burying

Remember, Daniel has been far away from home (Jerusalem) for seventy years. He's living in a place where there's great food and meat and
wine, and even a range of lotions to pamper the skin. It's a luxurious
place. It's the perfect place to bury the bad news. **He could eat loads
and drink loads and slap on the body lotion.** He could pretend to
be happy. But he won't.

Daniel hasn't forgotten his home. We know from chapter 6 that, when
he prays, he opens his windows towards Jerusalem. That's where his
heart is. So when he hears the news of how things are in Jerusalem, he
still feels the pain. He's still homesick for the *kingdom of God*.

Daniel isn't interested in burying the pain. In fact, Daniel is a man
who *decides to mourn*. As he receives this vision about Jerusalem, his
response is to face up to the harsh reality of the pain of this world.

By the rivers

In chapter 10 we're told that Daniel is standing on the bank of the
great river Tigris. Do you know what they did by the rivers of Babylon?

Psalm 137 tells us. It says this:

By the rivers of Babylon we sat and wept when we remembered
Zion (that's another name for Jerusalem).

Psalm 137 v 1

Daniel has come to the place of weeping. He has come to the place of sadness. He's not going to simply pretend that "every-little-thing-is-going-to-be-ok."

It isn't ok. Daniel's world isn't ok. Jerusalem, God's great city, isn't ok. It's in ruins. Daniel is devastated at what human sin has done to God's world.

He takes three weeks to think, to pray, to mourn. To remember that the kingdom of Babylon isn't his home. He could have just forgotten about Jerusalem and found comfort in the wine and lotions of Babylon. But he'll not find his comfort there. He chooses to mourn. He's homesick for Jerusalem.

No worm eating

Hold on. This sounds like Daniel might be feeling a bit sorry for himself.

No, that's not what's happening. He doesn't go down the garden and eat worms. He *mourns*. We have to understand the difference.

Wallowing is all about me. Poor me.

Mourning is all about God. It's being sad because God's world has been messed up. It's being sad because sin has spoiled things.

This is how Daniel coped with bad news.

He doesn't bury it. He doesn't wallow in it. He mourns over it.

It's not ok

When you turn on the TV, there's plenty of bad news. People starving, terrorists plotting, wars raging. This world isn't ok. How do we respond?

Don't ignore it. Don't wallow in it. Mourn over it.

As we go through life, we'll face bad news. People we love become sick. Things don't work out how we hoped. Relationships break down. Bullying, abuse, divorce. This world isn't ok. How will we cope?

We don't ignore it. We don't wallow in it. We mourn over it.

This is what makes *God's kingdom* so stunning. It gives us a way to deal with bad news. Please understand this: it's right to feel sad and cry over bad news. Because, as we cry, it reminds us that the *kingdom of the world* isn't our home. It makes us homesick for the *kingdom of God*.

Will you ask God now to help you learn how to mourn properly?

Why not **grab a piece of paper** and write down the things that make you sad about this world. Forget all the fake happiness that's around us, and engage with the reality of a broken world. Perhaps it's things about yourself. Or about your family and friends. Or about this world.

Write them down, but don't stop there—that would be moping. We're not into moping. We want to learn to mourn. So now, take those things on your list and talk to God about them. Be honest about how you feel.

As you do that, Jesus has a great promise for you:

> *Blessed are those who mourn for they will be comforted.*
> *Matthew 5 v 4*

In the midst of mourning, there's great comfort. **Not just a cuddle, a teddy bear and a cup of hot chocolate.** I am talking about real comfort. I am talking about someone who can actually fix the mess our sin has made.

The singer Michael Jackson sang a song called *Man in the Mirror*. In it he said that the way to make the world a better place is to look at, and change, yourself.

That's the best the *kingdom of the world* has to offer. Comfort is found as you look at yourself.

Daniel 10 shows us something far better. Don't look at the man (or woman) in the mirror. They can't fix the mess. There's no comfort there. Instead, **look at another man**. That's what Daniel sees as he mourns by the river. See for yourself:

> *I looked up and there before me was a man dressed in linen, with a belt of fine gold from Uphaz round his waist. His body was like topaz, his face like lightning, his eyes like flaming torches, his arms and legs like the gleam of burnished bronze, and his voice like the sound of a multitude.*
>
> *Daniel 10 v 5-6*

This is the man who can really comfort those who mourn. He's magnificent. Can you imagine him?

But who is this man?

See the Linen-Man

When you meet someone in the Bible dressed in linen, you're pretty safe to assume they're a priest. Linen was their thing (you can check that out in Leviticus 16 v 3-4). Plus, this man has a golden belt, another of the key bits of the priestly kit (see Exodus 39 v 5).

No doubt about it: we're looking at a priest. So what?

The priest's job was to deal with sin. They offered sacrifices in the temple, and God's anger towards his people would be turned away.

So the man Daniel saw can offer *real comfort* because he can deal with the *real problem*. **He's the Linen-Man who can deal with sin.**

Good news.

But this man is different from any other priest. He's also staggeringly powerful, like a mighty king. He's terrifying, with a face like lightning and burning eyes. It doesn't really matter what enemies you're up against if this man is on your side.

Do you see this man? He's the Priest who can deal with our sin. And he's the King who can bring security.

He's strong. He's awesome. He's terrifying. He's beautiful.

Daniel doesn't know the man's name, but we do. This is Jesus, the eternal Son of God. He's the Priest and he's the King. Daniel was shown a glimpse of him a few hundred years before Jesus was born in Bethlehem.

We have far too small a view of Jesus. We see him as a baby, or as a man, or dying on a cross. But that isn't the whole story. True comfort comes when we see that **the man who died in agony on a Roman cross is the same powerful man that Daniel saw**.

Here's what to do with your sadness and pain. Don't bury it and pretend to be happy. Instead, take your list of stuff and lift your eyes to Jesus. Allow him to fill your whole vision.

Worship him as the Priest who gave himself as the sacrifice that would pay for our sin. (By the way, do you know what Jesus was wrapped in as his body was placed in the tomb? Linen. See it in John 19 v 40. He's the Linen-Man—the Priest who deals with our sin.)

Worship him as the King who is stronger than all his enemies, even death. As the Priest-King, **Jesus alone has the power to fix this broken world** and bring in *God's great kingdom*.

It's when we see him that we find comfort in our mourning. Will you look with Daniel at this awesome Linen-Man?

Know your weakness

God's comfort isn't what you might expect...

Daniel collapses to the floor, and he's virtually dead.

> I was left alone, gazing at this great vision; I had no strength left, my face turned deathly pale and I was helpless. Then I heard him speaking, and as I listened to him, I fell into a deep sleep, my face to the ground.
>
> *Daniel 10 v 8-9*

When we see Jesus as he really is, it will leave us with a very deep sense of our own weakness.

Sometimes I go running. I don't enjoy running; I never *want* to go running; so I usually put on some music to inspire me. High-energy music gets me ready to go. It picks me up and gets my heart pumping. I feel fantastic.

Some people think that Jesus works like that. He makes you feel better about yourself; inspires you to be better; makes you feel good so that you can go out and achieve anything.

Umm... not so much.

Daniel saw Jesus, and now is virtually dead. Seeing this vision of Jesus doesn't inspire Daniel to go and change the world. In fact, he's even more aware of his own weakness. He cannot fix the problems. He cannot stop the weeping. He knows he's powerless.

Have you felt anything like that? Have you ever seen the sheer majesty of Jesus in a way that makes you feel how small and weak you are? **We have to let go of this idea that, with a bit of inspiring music, we can change the world.** Jesus is supremely strong. We're not. If we're going to experience his comfort, we have to feel our weakness.

Normally we try to avoid feeling weak. We cover our weaknesses and emphasise our strengths. But that's dangerous when it comes to Jesus. If we're obsessed with *our* strength, we'll never understand *his*.

But Daniel doesn't stay on the floor.

Experience his touch

In verse 10, we're told that this awesome Linen-Man stoops down and touches Daniel. He picks him up. That's a stunning thing to imagine.

Despite all the power, this man is bothered about Daniel. He knows Daniel's name.

This is how Jesus works. He comes to individuals and touches them. Read through the stories from Jesus' life in the Gospels. I bet it won't take you long to find one where Jesus touches someone. Jesus didn't just heal the crowds all at once—he comforted people one by one.

And so it is today. **He is interested in you.** He stoops down to lift you up.

That's why Jesus went down to the cross—in order to lift you up out of your sin and weakness.

Please read this carefully and let it sink in. As you bring your mourning and pain to Jesus; as you see him and feel your own weakness; he will lift you up. He will comfort you.

We don't need Jesus simply to inspire us. **We need him to pick us up out of the dirt and get us on our feet.** That's proper comfort.

So now Daniel is standing again. He's ready for the final stage of the comfort. He's ready to…

Hear the message

Do not be afraid, Daniel. Since the first day that you set your mind to gain understanding and to humble yourself before your God, your words were heard, and I have come in response to them.
Daniel 10 v 12

That's awesome! God both hears Daniel's words and responds to them.

There's something Daniel needs to know. The reason this world is so painful is that we're caught up in a war. God is establishing *his kingdom*. He's defeating the *kingdom of the world*.

Comfort comes when we understand this world properly.

But this is far too big to tag on to the end of this chapter. We're going to need a whole new chapter to explore it. So don't stop now. We're getting to the hardest bit of Daniel. I'll meet you there in a minute…

Chapter Eight:
Crashing waves

...the people who know their God shall stand firm.

Daniel 11 v 32 (ESV)

Please read Daniel 11

Are you sitting comfortably?

Actually... forget that. That's a rubbish question. Here's a better question for you as we head into Daniel chapter 11.

Are you standing firmly?

Sometimes things come crashing down on us. Stuff happens that threatens to knock us off our feet: things that are out of our control; things we don't want to happen; things we didn't expect to happen. The crashing waves will come. The question is: will you stand firm? Or will you be overwhelmed?

That's what Daniel 11 is really all about. Daniel is shown that things are going to get seriously stormy for God's people in Jerusalem. But don't panic.

In the eye of the storm there's a group of people who are able to stand firm. Verse 32 says that they are the ones who "know their God".

We've seen it through the life of Daniel. **Standing firm isn't about being brave and heroic—it's about knowing God.** It's knowing that he is the King whose kingdom will never be destroyed. Daniel knew it. Do we?

The man from Daniel's vision in chapter 10 is still speaking in chapter 11. He's telling Daniel about some terrifying waves that are going to hit God's people. He's telling Daniel so that the people will be ready and stand their ground. We've heard these things before, but God's people really need to be ready…

The unseen war

In case you've missed it so far, there's a war raging. It's a war between the *kingdom of God* and the *kingdom of the world*. It's a war that's happening on earth. But at the end of chapter 10, Daniel is shown that this war is also happening in the unseen heavenly realms.

Although many might dismiss the idea of a war in heaven, the Bible says that it's very real. There's an unseen spiritual world of angels and demons. This is why Daniel is told in chapter 10 about a character called Michael. He's an angelic being—called a "prince" (v 13)—who leads an army of angels in defending Jerusalem. He's fighting against the enemy "princes" of Persia and Greece. They are demonic beings associated with the *kingdom of the world*.

Daniel needs to understand that there are unseen evil forces fighting against God. There are powers of darkness that seek to destroy those who belong to *God's kingdom*. And we need to understand it, too.

It's a war that continues to this day. Ephesians 6 says that Christians are caught up in a struggle…

> …*against the powers of this dark world and against the spiritual forces of evil in the heavenly realms.*
>
> *Ephesians 6 v 12*

No wonder life feels so hard sometimes. No wonder we get battered by waves crashing around us. If we belong to *God's kingdom*, there is an enemy who wants to destroy us. He'll lie to us; he'll tempt us; he'll spoil stuff; he'll offer us things to draw us away. We need to see the war and stand firm.

Ephesians 6 goes on to say:

> *Therefore put on the full armour of God, so that when the day of evil comes, you may be able to stand your ground, and after you have done everything, to stand.*
>
> *Ephesians 6 v 13*

So, there's a war in heaven. It's vicious. But with our confidence in God and his power, we'll stand firm. We need to know God's truth to combat the lies. We need to see the beauty of Jesus to combat the empty temptations of the world. We need to see the goodness of God so that we don't fall for the enemy's attempt to destroy us.

But the war isn't only in the heavenly realms.

The war on earth

The war in heaven means that there are crashing waves on earth. The two things are connected. God's people need to be ready. They need to know their God.

Here's a very quick tour of what Daniel is told in chapter 11. As I describe it, listen out for the crashing waves.

History alert: we already know that after the Babylonian Empire, comes the Persian Empire. Then, after the Persians comes the Greek Empire. That's the mighty king who is talked about in verse 3. (He's Alexander the Great again, in case you were wondering.) When he dies, his kingdom is spilt into four—and chapter 11 focuses on two of those kingdoms. There's a king up in the North (helpfully called the king of the North) and a king in the South (helpfully called the king of the South).

The city of Jerusalem (God's city) is caught right in the middle. Remember that. It really matters.

The king of the North and the king of the South start off on friendly (ish) terms with a wedding. It doesn't last long. Here come the waves.

The king of the South goes crashing up and attacks the king of the North, and nicks loads of his stuff.

Then the king of the North goes crashing down like a great flood to the South, but it doesn't go well and he has to run back home. Then the North has another go with a huge army.

The king of the South comes out to fight back, and the king of the North loses. The king of the South is happy for a while ("Yay, I'm the strongest"), but then the king of the North attacks again with an even bigger army. He wins.

Remember Jerusalem? All this is going on around them. It's scary stuff. It would be easy to lose your nerve and join up with whichever king seems to be winning at the time.

So, the king of the North is top dog now. But then he dies and is replaced by king of the North mark 2. But he dies too. So we move on to the king of the North mark 3. Are you keeping up with this?

Then things take a more sinister twist. Suddenly, **Jerusalem becomes the focus of attention**. The waves don't just crash *around* Jerusalem. They come crashing down upon the city.

When the king of the North loses a battle with the king of the South, listen to what happens:

> Then he (king of the North mark 3) will turn back and vent his fury against the holy covenant (that's God's people in Jerusalem). He will return and show favour to those who forsake the holy covenant.
>
> His armed forces will rise up to desecrate the temple fortress and will abolish the daily sacrifice. Then they will set up the abomination that causes desolation. With flattery he will corrupt those who have violated the covenant, but the people who know their God will firmly resist him.
>
> Daniel 11 v 30-32

This king of the North attacks Jerusalem. He uses violence to attack the city—but also speaks nicely to people, trying to convince them to abandon God and join him.

It will be a tough time for Jerusalem, and they will need to stand firm as the waves crash down on them.

This king of the North is the worst of the lot. He sets himself up against God. **But only for as long as God allows.** (Remember, God has all these kings on a lead.)

For one final time the king of the South attacks the king of the North, and the king of the North sweeps out to meet him. This is it. This is the end. Just when it looks as if the king of the North is unstoppable, chapter 11 ends like this:

> He will pitch his royal tents between the seas at the beautiful holy mountain. Yet he will come to his end, and no one will help him.
>
> Daniel 11 v 45

And that's it. Game over.

It sounds complicated, but don't get stressed by all the detail. Hold on to the main things. If we're going to join *God's kingdom*, it isn't going to be easy. There'll be waves that crash all around us. We are caught up in a war.

Just like the city of Jerusalem in Daniel's day, God's church today will be battered by waves. Jesus warned his followers just as he warned Daniel.

In Mark 13 v 13, Jesus says:

> *Everyone will hate you because of me, but the one who stands firm to the end will be saved.*

It's the same warning: it's going to be tough. Sometimes there'll be waves that crash around us that are out of our control—people fighting one another—between nations, in families, in friendship groups. These waves can be frightening, but stand firm.

Even as I write this, Christians in Iraq are having to flee their homes because of fighting that's going on around them. It's scary. They need to know their God and stand firm with their confidence in *his kingdom*.

Sometimes, the waves will be aimed directly at us. People will get angry about what we believe. People don't want to hear about Jesus. This is strong stuff. Jesus says that people will hate those who choose to be part of *his kingdom*. **If we don't hear that warning, we're going to be knocked off our feet when people give us a hard time.**

It's tough to stand firm when "clever scientists" say that believing in God is stupid. It's tough to stand firm when you might lose your friends and be known as a loser. It's tough to stand firm when your family thinks you're weird. It's tough to stand firm when your boyfriend threatens to dump you for being a Christian. It's tough to stand firm when you feel like you're missing out.

It all feels pretty risky. It all feels a bit dangerous.

No one likes being in danger. We all try to find security. We all look for things that make us feel safe.

My eldest son used to have a Winnie-the-Pooh toy that made him feel safe. Crazy, huh? How can a soft toy ever keep him safe? I don't think it was a ninja-trained soft toy. It was powerless. But it made him feel safe.

Before you're too quick to judge, think about your "Winnie-the-Poohs". What is it that you think will keep you secure and standing firm?

An education? A relationship? A nice family? A job? A career? Popularity? All these things are what make us feel safe. But they aren't up to the job. If they are our ultimate security, we're in great danger when the waves crash around us.

The only way to stand firm is to know your God. To know that his kingdom is the one that lasts for ever.

There's a very important word in Daniel 11. God's people are described as the people of the "covenant" (see verses 28 and 30). A covenant is a promise. God has made a covenant with his people. The heart of his promise is this:

You will be my people, and I will be your God.

Jeremiah 30 v 22

That's where true security is to be found. God has promised. God has committed himself to his people. **He will not let them down, no matter how scary the waves become.** Knowing God means knowing the promise he has made to his people.

The king of the North and the king of the South kept building bigger armies and stronger fortresses. That's what made them feel safe. That's where their confidence lay. That was their "Winnie-the-Pooh". But the armies got defeated and the fortresses got smashed down.

But here's the cool thing. Do you know how God is described?

> *The Lord is my rock, my fortress and my deliverer; my God is my rock, in whom I take refuge, my shield and the horn of my salvation, my stronghold.*
> *Psalm 18 v 2*

When the waves crash, here is the place of safety. Standing firm means knowing God as my fortress. It doesn't mean the waves aren't scary. It doesn't mean everything will be easy. But it does mean we're safe.

God's promise to us comes through Jesus. His death on the cross is our guarantee of safety. To all who believe in him, he says: *You are my people and I am your God.*

Do you know him? Is he your fortress? When the waves strike, do you stand firm?

You can tell where your confidence lies by finishing this sentence: "I think my life will be ok because…"

Whatever you put in the blank is your "Winnie-the-Pooh". What is it? Do you see what it is in your life? Maybe not an army and a fortress, but there'll be something that makes you feel safe.

We need to replace "Winnie-the-Pooh" with the great God of Heaven.

Remember Daniel facing the lion's den? Where was his confidence? This is what we were told:

> *And when Daniel was lifted from the den, no wound was found on him, because he had trusted in his God.*
>
> *Daniel 6 v 23*

If you feel the waves crashing around you, stand firm. **Know that God will never let you go. Know that God won't fail you.** Know that God will bring you safely to *his eternal kingdom*. Know it because he has promised it. Know it because Jesus died and rose again to make it possible. It may feel scary for a while. It may hurt. But God will bring you safely through to *his everlasting kingdom*.

There's much more about that kingdom as we head towards the end of the book… It's an amazing ending.

Chapter Nine:
What a finish

How long will it be before these
astonishing things are fulfilled?   Daniel 12 v 6

Please read Daniel chapter 12

Welcome to The End.

Not just the end of this book, but a vision of *The End of Time.*

The vision that began back in Daniel Chapter 10 reaches its amazing conclusion here in Chapter 12. The Linen-Man is still speaking. So this isn't simply wishful thinking—it's spoken by the man who has the power to bring it about.

It all starts with these words,

> *At that time Michael, the great prince who protects your people,*
> *will arise. There will be a time of distress such as has not happened*
> *from the beginning of nations until then. But at that time your*
> *people—everyone whose name is found written in the book—will*
> *be delivered.*
>
> *Daniel 12 v 1*

Here we go. Get this clear Daniel.

Daniel is clearly shown that things are going to be bad. There'll be great distress. We've already seen some of that. Think of the beasts of chapter 7, the horns of chapter 8, and the waves of chapter 11. All that sounded pretty bad. But then, in chapter 12, Daniel is told that he should expect things to **get harder**.

All this talk of distress doesn't fit with how we normally think. We assume that things are supposed to be easy in this world. We think, when things are hard, that everything has gone wrong.

Let me give you some silly examples. I go on a journey in my car—I hit a traffic jam—I am annoyed because I assume the journey was supposed to be easy. How dare these other cars decide to drive at the same time as me? It's outrageous.

I was out for coffee with a friend the other day and a bird pooed on me. I was angry. I was mortally offended. This should not happen—it's wrong. Things are supposed to go well, not badly.

I'm not supposed to get sick. I'm not supposed to suffer pain. I'm not supposed to suffer at all. That's how we think. And it's a big problem.

It means we'll quickly get disappointed and disillusioned with life. I meet loads of people who moan that life is hard. We're all tempted to grumble, aren't we?

"I'm tired. I'm stressed. Everything is going wrong. My life is falling apart."

Listen: life is hard. We live in the time of distress. We live in a sinful world. Things are broken. People do evil things. Stuff breaks. Disasters happen. Cancer strikes. Car accidents destroy families. I know it's painful. I know it hurts. But it's what God says this world will be like. There's a war going on. The *kingdom of the world* is a place of distress.

Without God, this is it. You just have to deal with the distress. **You live. You suffer. You die. The end. Get over it.**

But.

Daniel is told that distress isn't the end of the story.

Distress is followed by deliverance. At the end of time, God's people will be delivered. He has their names written in his book and they will be set free. They will be rescued from the distressing world.

If you belong to his kingdom, then he knows your name. It's written in his book. He won't forget anyone. You'll be brought through the distress to a place of security and safety.

It's like when a baby is born. Sort of. There's much pain and distress—it hurts. But then comes the delivery. The baby is born, the pain is finished and there's great joy in the new life.

Distress followed by *deliverance*.

Knowing that deliverance is coming helps us to cope with the distress of this world. Knowing the future changes how I deal with the present. We do this all the time in small ways.

You put up with the distress of a boring job because you're thinking about the money you'll be paid. You put up with early morning training sessions because you're thinking of the gold medal you'll win (this isn't an example from personal experience, I'm guessing…).

You get the point. **The only way to cope with present distress is to be absolutely confident that deliverance is coming.**

Jesus is the great example of that. How could Jesus cope with the distress and agony of death on a cross? He knew that a great deliverance was coming. He knew that he would be raised to new life—delivered from the grave; freed from the agony.

And as you trust in him, you will be too.

Pain and distress usually make us focus on the present. If we're not careful, we'll become bitter and self-obsessed. We'll grumble and complain that everything has gone wrong.

But it's a magnificent thing when you see distress having the opposite effect; when it makes people fix their eyes on the future; when it fills people with a longing for the *kingdom of God* rather than the *kingdom of this world*.

Have you ever seen that? Have you ever seen someone who is trusting Jesus in the middle of suffering?

It isn't ignoring the pain. It isn't keeping calm and carrying on. It's confidence that deliverance is coming.

Distress is real, but it isn't the end for God's people. We look forward to a greater hope and a greater future.

Daniel needed to know that. Jesus needed to know that. And so do we.

Not only is our world a painful place, it's temporary too.

The temporary is followed by the everlasting

I love a bowl of ice cream. But I can't completely enjoy it because I know that it's going to end. Every spoonful I enjoy is spoiled by the knowledge that I've got one less spoonful left. **It's gone too soon.**

It's the terrible thing about pleasure in our world. We long for the summer holidays;

we plan and we dream about being away from work; but then suddenly it's all over. We're back in the classroom or at work. **It's gone too soon.**

Nothing lasts—our health, our youth, our eyesight, our friendships—they're gone too soon. They race past and we can't keep hold of them. Everything good about this world is spoiled by the knowledge that it doesn't last for ever. It will be gone. We will die. But there's something everlasting—and that's what really counts.

Look at the words of verse 2. They describe an extraordinary thing that will happen at the end:

> *Multitudes who sleep in the dust of the earth will awake: some to everlasting life, others to shame and everlasting contempt. Those who are wise will shine like the brightness of the heavens, and those who lead many to righteousness, like the stars for ever and ever.*
> *Daniel 12 v 2-3*

There's a day coming when all those who have died will be raised again. Life in this world is temporary, but there's a future coming for all people that is everlasting.

Daniel is told that death isn't the end of the story for anyone. A great resurrection day is coming when all will rise. And they will be raised to an everlasting reality. Either it will be to everlasting life, or it will be to everlasting shame and contempt.

Can you see that this everlasting future is far more important than the temporary stuff we get so obsessed about?

There are only two futures. Both are everlasting. Everyone who has ever lived will spend forever in one of these futures.

One is unspeakably terrible. And one unspeakably wonderful.

For those who have lived for the *kingdom of the world*, there's a terrible future. For those who have lived ignoring Jesus, the king of *God's kingdom*, there'll be shame and contempt for ever. This is a place of everlasting punishment. It's a place the Bible calls hell.

Jesus warns of exactly the same thing. Because of his great love for humanity, he warns us of this horrific reality. He says that some will "go away to eternal punishment" (Matthew 25 v 46).

Rescue

By nature, I deserve to face this punishment. I've often lived for this world. I've often done what I know God says is wrong. But **this is the whole reason Jesus came**—to save me from the shame and contempt of hell.

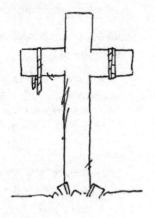

On the cross, Jesus took upon himself my shame and my contempt. He took upon himself my punishment. He took upon himself my hell. It's described in the Bible like this:

> But he was pierced for our transgressions,
> he was crushed for our iniquities;
> the punishment that brought us peace was on him,
> and by his wounds we are healed.
>
> *Isaiah 53 v 5*

This means that, although I deserve everlasting shame, I can instead receive everlasting life.

And that's a wonderful future. It's described in Daniel 12 v 3 as shining like the brightness of the heavens. All the distress and pain are finished. I will be raised to life that never ends. No more death. No more tears. My decaying body will be transformed to a glorious body.

My hurt and frustration and disappointment will melt into inexpressible and glorious joy.

Go and read Revelation 21 v 1-5. Enjoy it. Believe it. I deserve everlasting punishment, but instead, through Jesus, I am promised everlasting life.

You've got to understand that weeping is followed by joy; that despair is followed by dancing; that heartbreak is followed by healing; that pain is followed by peace; that frustration is followed by freedom. **This is what lasts. Only this.**

Who cares?

In the light of this everlasting future, you get thinking. Who cares what car you drive, or clothes you wear, or holidays you take? They're all temporary. Instead we will want to **get ready for what is everlasting**.

Being ready for that day is simple. You don't have to pass an exam, or go through some ritual. You get ready by joining *God's kingdom*. Admit you've messed up. Believe that Jesus died for you. Turn to him as your King.

If you've never done that, then why not do it now? You could use these simple words as a prayer.

Heavenly Father,

I admit I've lived life ignoring you. I admit I deserve to face your punishment.

Thank you for Jesus. Thank you that on the cross the punishment I deserve was placed on him. I want to belong to your eternal kingdom. I want to invest my life in the only kingdom that lasts for ever. Please help me.

Amen

It changes everything. We can enjoy the good things God gives, but we won't become obsessed by money and fashion and education and work and partying and sport. We'll use those things to make *God's Kingdom* known.

How can you use the gifts God has given you to serve him rather than to serve yourself? Get some bigger ambitions. Forget being rich, being famous, being successful. They're too small. They don't last. Dream of how God might use you to spread *his kingdom*.

If you're good at cutting people's hair, then work hard at it. Do the best job you can. You'll meet loads of people. You can bring honour to God as you do your job well. Use your gifts to make Jesus known.

If you're good at making money, then work hard and make loads of it. Make as much as you can and then use it for the glory of *God's kingdom*. You could fund people to take the good news overseas. You could help plant churches. That's exciting. **Do you see how it changes things?**

If sport is your thing, then pursue it for God's glory. Don't just dream of a five-year career in top-level sport. Dream of using your sport to reach hundreds of people in all sorts of places with the message of *God's kingdom*.

You can work this out. God has created you to live for him. He'll use you to establish *his kingdom* on earth, wherever you are.

It won't be easy. You'll face pressure to give up on God and invest everything in this world. Daniel did. But he stood firm. And so must you. Be courageous because *God's kingdom* is awesome.

One more thing to get clear before we leave Daniel…

Daniel wants to know when this is all going to happen. That's what someone asks in verse 6:

How long will it be before these astonishing things are fulfilled?

The answer is:

It will be for a time, times and half a time. When the power of the holy people has been finally broken, all these things will be completed.

Daniel 12 v 7

Not quite what Daniel was looking for. He isn't told a time and a date, just a phrase that seems to make no sense. It's God's way of saying: "I've got this under control Daniel. I know when the end will come. It's in hand. You don't need to know the details."

At the moment when it looks like all is lost, then the end will come. No questions. God has it in hand.

Don't panic. Stand firm. You won't be disappointed.

Epilogue

As the book of Daniel ends he still has more questions.

> *I heard, but I did not understand. So I asked, "My lord, what will the outcome of all this be?"*
>
> Daniel 12 v 8

He's still a bit muddled on some of the details. He wants to keep asking his questions. But he's told in verse 9:

> *Go your way, Daniel, because the words are rolled up and sealed until the time of the end.*

Daniel knows enough. He has been shown extraordinary things. He has seen clearly the overwhelming power and beauty of *God's kingdom*. He has seen the great future God has promised. He has seen that the suffering of this world will be replaced with the joy and glory of *God's eternal kingdom*. He has seen enough.

He doesn't know everything. He still has questions. But he knows enough. Now it's time for him to get on and live it. It's time for him to stand firm, hold on and not despair. "Go your way, Daniel."

Daniel knows enough and so do we.

God doesn't provide answers to all the questions we might have. But he has told us enough for us to get on and live for *his kingdom*.

Through this book, we've been shown the brutal reality of the *kingdom of the world*. A world where power is abused, where nothing lasts, and where death puts an end to even the most powerful kings.

And we have seen the majesty of the *kingdom of God*: where God rules, where his people are kept safe, and where the glory will last for ever and ever.

Haven't you seen enough? You may still have questions. Of course you do. But isn't it time to get on and live this life?

When the waves crash and you feel like giving up, **stand firm**. When the temptations come and you can feel your heart being pulled away, **hold your nerve**.

The *kingdom of God* is better. It's the only kingdom worth investing in. Let's get on with it.

What next?

It's been quite a journey through the book of Daniel. And it doesn't end here. The journey continues as you live out what you've learned.

It would be good to have a think about how you want to move forward.

- What's the biggest thing you've discovered about God and *his kingdom*?
- What are you going to ask God to help you to change?
- What are you going to do about it?

It won't be easy, and you'll need help along the way. You'll need some good Christian mates to help you (just as Daniel had Shadrach, Meshach, and Abednego). You'll need to keep learning more about *God's great kingdom* from the Bible. Why not try some of these resources…

Start: These Bible notes will help you understand the basic message of the Bible—who Jesus is, why he came and what he wants us to do as a result.

Engage: For those who want to dig into the Bible regularly—great questions and help for understanding God's book.

Daniel stood firm for seventy years. **Will you?**

thegoodbook
COMPANY
Opening up the Bible

At The Good Book Company, we are dedicated to helping Christians and local churches grow. We believe that God's growth process always starts with hearing clearly what he has said to us through his timeless word—the Bible.

Ever since we opened our doors in 1991, we have been striving to produce resources that honour God in the way the Bible is used. We have grown to become an international provider of user-friendly resources to the Christian community, with believers of all backgrounds and denominations using our Bible studies, books, evangelistic resources, DVD-based courses and training events.

We want to equip ordinary Christians to live for Christ day by day, and churches to grow in their knowledge of God, their love for one another, and the effectiveness of their outreach.

Call us for a discussion of your needs or visit one of our local websites for more information on the resources and services we provide.

UK & Europe: www.thegoodbook.co.uk
North America: www.thegoodbook.com
Australia: www.thegoodbook.com.au
New Zealand: www.thegoodbook.co.nz

UK & Europe: 0333 123 0880
North America: 866 244 2165
Australia: (02) 6100 4211
New Zealand (+64) 3 343 1990

www.christianityexplored.org

Our partner site is a great place for those exploring the Christian faith, with a clear explanation of the good news, powerful testimonies and answers to difficult questions.

One life. What's it all about?